TAKING
A ZERO

TAKING A ZERO

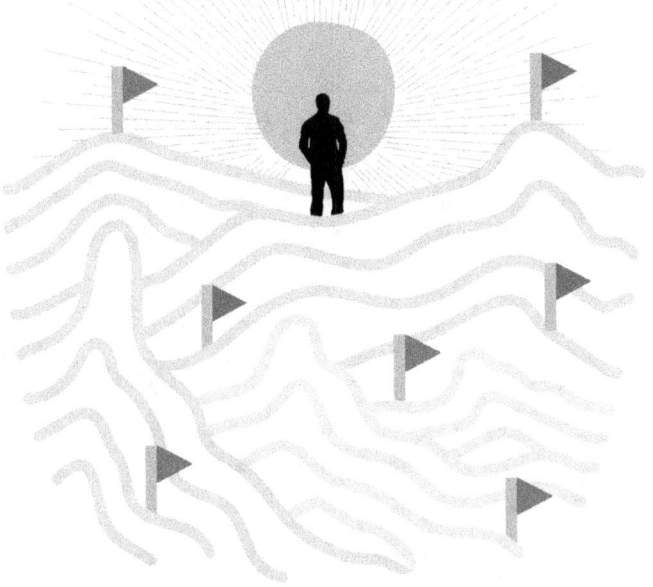

*Imagining the Stages
and Gauges of Discipleship*

RICK SHAFER

Scripture quotations are from Revised Standard Version
of the Bible, copyright © 1946, 1952, and 1971 National
Council of the Churches of Christ in the United States of
America. All rights reserved worldwide.

Printed in the United States of America

Library of Congress Control Number: 2022917666

Paperback ISBN: 979-8-9866949-6-2
Ebook ISBN: 979-8-9866949-7-9

Storylines United Media
Wilmington, North Carolina USA
storylinesunited.com

For Elizabeth.

I journey His Greatness

to trembling's door.

There

meet His Goodness greeting:

"Do not fear, my child.

Approach

my throne with confidence."

My Father is fear extinguished;

Perfect Peace is my reward.

ACKNOWLEDGMENTS

My family has been part of Port City Community Church since 2002, and I joined the church staff in 2013. All these years, I have been inspired by our church's mission and vision:

To reach people and help them walk with God (mission) so that we experience *Life with God together for the world* (vision).

Having this focus, we've needed to learn how to assess effectiveness and progress. This has become one of my favorite projects. Thank you to Senior Pastor Mike Ashcraft, our church's leadership, staff, and people. None of this would be possible without experimentation, patience, and resolve.

Thanks to my wife, Elizabeth, for being with me in this for so many years. Your 'regular life' perspective is welcoming to all who abide with Christ, regardless of their station or vocation in this world. You remind me that Jesus is worthy of our everyday moments.

And thanks to God – Father, Son, and Spirit – whose work in this world is always for redemption, reconciliation, and restoration. Sometimes that seems big and broad. But right now, it feels close and personal. I want what you want.

INTRODUCTION

In my first book, *Companion Planted*, my objective was to orient disciples to their discipleship. In this book, I want to share ways for disciples and their guides to celebrate progress. I think of discipleship progress in terms of depth rather than destination. And I see discipleship primarily as a new belonging expressed in new behaviors.

God has rescued us from one dominion and has resettled us in his own (Col. 1:13). Everything has been made new in us and for us (2 Cor. 5:17). Now, we are engaged in the process of this 'new' becoming more normal, less foreign. We are learning to place our trust in a new Sovereign – who also reveals himself to us as Father. As this trust works itself into our thoughts, choices, and behaviors, we are increasingly living by faith. Living by faith is the aim of our life as Jesus' disciples.

If the title of this book suggests taking a zero on a test, then please do it with intention. The person who works hard *for* God's love and favor may need to take a zero and begin living *with* him by grace. But this book is about something else. There's a concept in thru-hiking called 'taking a zero'. A zero day is a pause. It's a day with no push forward on the journey. Maybe the weather is terrible, or the hiker's body needs recovery. If there's a town nearby, enjoying a hot shower and visiting the laundromat might be on the agenda.

Examine yourselves to see whether you are holding to your faith. Test yourselves. Do you not realize that Jesus Christ is in you? – unless indeed you fail to meet the test! (2 Cor. 13:5)

Taking a pause spiritually is about making time for reflection, assessment, and adjustment. For some, this might be an annual exercise practiced around a birthday or near year's end. Others may practice a daily *examen*. Associated with St. Ignatius and Jesuits – the spiritual discipline of *examen* is given for reflecting on each day and discerning God's direction. *Examen* is a beneficial discipline; many resources are available to guide you. This book's idea of *Taking a Zero* could be used as a daily *examen*. But it can also be used to assess formation over more extended periods. Use it personally or use it corporately.

As an engineer, I was trained to measure things. Thermometers, scales, clocks, and the like, help me see and evaluate position and progress. As I write this, our grandson is in his first year of life. Monthly he comes home from the doctor with a chart showing his percentile scores in height, weight, and head circumference. Those metrics say something about his progress. Other metrics attempt to quantify cognitive, social and emotional, language, and physical milestones. These measures don't tell us everything. There's a lot more going on that we can't measure. But they are helpful.

After college, I designed and built small chemical plants for a living. Included in those designs were sensors and feedback loops that allowed me to *monitor* a plant's operation. Much of my work involved relating processes and sensors to finished product quality. Discipleship processes, like chemical processes, are complex. Really, people are much more complex than molecules. However good, our discipleship processes and metrics won't guarantee predictable, precise outcomes. But even general markers can be useful. And what's the alternative anyway? Without assessment, how can we know that what we're doing is helpful?

If you have read *Companion Planted*, you know that I believe the disciple's target – our finished product – is a life of faith working through love (Gal. 5:6). I define faith as *trust that's able to take a step* – trust in God that reorders our actual lived life. How are we moving toward this? And how can we evaluate our progress?

In Part 1 of this book, I use one of Jesus' most familiar stories to think about *stages* of discipleship. There are different ways to look at discipleship stages. Here I suggest one way that draws from a parable.

In Part 2, I offer five *gauges* of discipleship. Not discipleship scales calibrated to tenths and hundredths. Just indicators. Jesus himself gave us some indicators:

"By this all men will know that you are my disciples, if you have love for one another." (John 13:35)

And,

"Either make the tree good, and its fruit good; or make the tree bad, and its fruit bad; for the tree is known by its fruit." (Matt. 12:33)

The Gauges give disciples some indicators to reflect on, pray over, and work toward. And they provide pastors, mentors, and guides something to watch.

STAGES, GAUGES, AND PATHWAYS

In this book, I will share four stages and five gauges of 'discipleship to formation'. Discipleship is the investment. Formation is what we long for – to become more like Christ and his kingdom. The process of discipleship is often thought about in terms of pathways. When asked: "What is your discipleship pathway?" I answer in a surprising way. Let me explain.

My definition of discipleship is *training myself and others* (B) *to be trained by Christ* (A). There are two parts to this definition. Many think of the (B) part as a discipleship pathway. It usually consists of catechism or a series of studies, Sunday School, small groups, quiet times, serving, giving, and missions efforts. To the extent that these activities and environments help people with the (A) part, they are very helpful. But the (B) part should never stand on its own. B-Part discipleship must serve A-Part discipleship.

Then Jesus told his disciples, "If any man would come after me, let him deny himself and take up his cross and follow me." (Matt. 16:24)

Following Jesus – being trained by him – is A-Part discipleship. Jesus' discipleship pathway is: deny yourself, take up your cross every day, and follow him. This is my answer to: "What is your discipleship pathway?". However our discipleship programs are configured, our goal is to be with Jesus as his students. He is our Master Trainer. The Stages and Gauges anticipate B-Part discipleship but require A-Part discipleship. Our first question is: Are we enrolled in Jesus' training? Then we can follow with: Do our activities and environments facilitate Jesus' training?

PART 1

IMAGINING *the* STAGES *of* DISCIPLESHIP

A few years ago, sitting in a rocking chair on the front porch and reading a familiar parable in Matthew, I noticed four stages of discipleship. It was the Parable of the Sower or Parable of the Soils in Matthew 13, also found in Mark 4 and Luke 8. In the Matthew account, Jesus starts this way:

> A sower went out to sow. And as he sowed, some seeds fell along the path, and the birds came and devoured them. Other seeds fell on rocky ground, where they had not much soil, and immediately they sprang up, since they had no depth of soil, but when the sun rose they were scorched; and since they had no root they withered away. Other seeds fell upon thorns, and the thorns grew up and choked them. Other seeds fell on good soil and brought forth grain, some a hundred-fold, some sixty, some thirty. (Matt. 13:3b-8)

In response, the disciples ask Jesus why he always speaks in parables because they find his stories hard to understand. I remember reading once that of the 183 times Jesus was asked a direct question, he answered directly only three of those times.[1] Might God have a bigger purpose for our relationship with him than dispensing answers to questions? In this instance, Jesus goes go on to explain.

This story is commonly used to test the condition of our hearts. How are we postured or positioned to nurture the message of God's kingdom? But this day, in a rocking chair, I saw *stages* of discipleship.

[1] *Jesus Is the Question: The 307 Questions Jesus Asked and the 3 He Answered*, Martin B. Copenhaver, © Sept. 2, 2014, Abingdon Press.

THE MESSAGE

Before we get to the soils, we should see that there's a seed and a sower. Jesus explains to us what the seed is. It's the word of God – the message of his Kingdom. Jesus and the Gospel writers are telling us that there's a message God wants to share. The Greek word is *logos*. *Logos* means *message* or *revealed wisdom*. It's what God has to say. When we refer to the Scriptures as God's word, we're saying they are God's message. When we read in John's gospel that Jesus is the Word, we hear John saying that Jesus is God's Message. Jesus is what God has to say.

The seed in this story is God's message of his kingdom. His message is found throughout Scripture, including Jesus' life, example, and teaching. God's names and laws in the Old Testament reveal him. New Testament writers show us how God's message was to be lived out in the early churches. Psalm 19 tells us that Creation, too, declares the message of God.

What is the scope of God's message? It might be bigger than you think. The extent of his kingdom is vast. Jesus is King! He rules over a kingdom you and I are invited to inhabit with him. This kingdom gives us an identity. It has a culture and a purpose in the world. God intends the seeds being sown in this parable to grow into mighty plants

– plants that will flourish and bear fruit in abundance if they are well tended. But God's *logos* doesn't come all at once. God reveals his message at a pace we can absorb.

In this story, there's also a sower. Is God the sower? Are we the sower? I think the answer is yes! If the seed is God's message, he must be the Original Sower. But we see in 1 Corinthians 3:6-8 that the apostle Paul planted, but God brought the growth. God plants, and we plant with him. Working together, the beautiful messages of his kingdom are sown.

It's the nature of plants to reproduce. A plant's fruit contains seeds for more fruit down the line. If your life and mine are the products (produce) of Kingdom seeds sown in us, we should aspire to be fruitful and sow seeds – the message of God's kingdom – in others. As sowers who co-labor with the Sower, we cast his seeds (messages) on soil. In his explanation of this parable, Jesus tells about four soils that receive the seeds. Let's imagine each soil as a stage of a journey – a long hike. As we do, periodically Take a Zero and reflect on your own position, progress, and direction.

THE SEEKER STAGE

When any one hears the word of the kingdom and does not understand it, the evil one comes and snatches away what is sown in his heart; this is what was sown along the path. (Matt. 13:19)

The first stage I draw from this parable I call the Seeker stage. Maybe think of this as approaching the trailhead. Perhaps you have been thinking about beginning your life with Christ. God has been. He has been trying to reach you. Or maybe you sense God is revealing something more of himself or his kingdom.

The Seeker in Jesus' story receives a particular message of God's kingdom – a revelation. We might imagine that if the seed were to penetrate the Seeker's hard surface, the soil beneath might be able to sustain life. But there's a problem. Maybe the Seeker is hard-hearted, but Jesus seems to be saying something more: the Seeker doesn't *understand*. It could be that Seekers don't understand because they're not open to understanding. It could be that they've received other messages of the kingdom and are resisting this one. Maybe they're not making enough effort to understand. Or it could be that, despite their best efforts, they just simply don't understand. In verses 13-14, Jesus quotes Isaiah, saying their hearts have grown dull, their ears are tired of hearing, and their eyes have closed. Whatever the reason, an Enemy steals the message that's just sitting there on the surface. It's lost before it's understood and has a chance to take root.

As churches that welcome and give space to Seekers, what can we do culturally to help them encounter the message of God's kingdom *with understanding*? We will naturally think of the sermon. But what about our other environments and interactions? How can we encourage questions and patient dialog? Are there creative ways we can help Seekers see what faith looks like when it's lived out? Will we pray for Seekers' hearts to come alive, their ears to hear, their eyes to open, and their minds to understand?

If you see yourself as a Seeker, keep seeking. Be on the lookout for God's message. Spend time in quiet. Listen for the Spirit's still, small voice. As we've already seen, Creation declares something of God's kingdom. In the universe, we see vastness. We see design. We see beauty. God is revealing himself in his creation. God may be speaking to you in other ways, too: something you read, a sermon, an act of kindness, some other experience – good or bad.

Consider that God is *pursuing you*. The Bible tells us that while we were still rebels, Christ died for us (Rom. 5:8) and that we love because God loved us first (1 John 4:19). Everyone who has a relationship with God entered that relationship in response to God's pursuit and by his grace. The same is true for our growth. God is trying to reveal himself and his ways to us.

Allow the possibility that you don't fully understand the message you have received. Be humble. Even those first disciples who walked most closely with Jesus often didn't understand. Find someone reliable to process with.

And take God's message to heart. Let it penetrate. Chew on it and allow it to shape you. Don't let the Enemy rob you of what God has to say.

If you have the privilege of helping Seekers, be a good example. Be people who have personally received messages of God's kingdom – the manifold wisdom of God (Eph. 3:10) – and have taken them to heart.

Try to explain the message of the kingdom clearly and patiently. We're often encouraged to declare – to proclaim – the gospel. This parable shows us that it's better to help people *understand* the gospel. Our work isn't done until people understand.

And look for ways to remove barriers to belief. Life in God's kingdom is a life of faith that involves trust. People need to see evidence of God's trustworthiness and that the way of Jesus is true. Does he really change lives? Do Jesus' followers really look like him?

THE STARTER STAGE

As for what was sown on rocky ground, this is he who hears the word and immediately receives it with joy; yet he has no root in himself, but endures for a while, and when tribulation or persecution arises on account of the word, immediately he falls away. (Matt. 13:20-21)

The next stage I see in this parable is the Starter. This is the hiker on the beginning section of a journey with God's Kingdom message – a particularly steep part of the trail. The Starter has received a seed of revelation. They understand. Their soil is perfect for germination. It's getting good sunshine. It's warm. And there aren't many competitors. In these conditions, the seed sprouts quickly, and the plant grows fast. But again, there's a problem. In these conditions, the plant can quickly grow bigger than its depth can support. The searing sun can wilt it. A strong wind can uproot it.

As churches that help Starters, what can we do culturally to encourage depth? How can we reframe the very *concept* of depth – away from sampling information and toward deeper rootedness? Real depth is what sustains our faith when trials, disappointments, and even persecutions come.

If you are a Starter, remember the vitality you have

right now. What are the emotions surrounding your relationship with Jesus? Relief? Gratitude? Joy? Hope? Do you feel renewed? Do you feel clean? Write about what you're feeling. Mark this moment so you will remember this 'first love' later on. (Rev. 2:4)

Be patient. Pace yourself. Some – especially new believers – try to get involved in everything all at once. The unfortunate consequence of this is that they tend to burn out. And burnout can lead to falling away. Too much activity can be an enemy of depth. Give yourself space to think and to process with God and others. Yes, get connected. Participate somehow. But take it slow. Get involved at a pace you can sustain. You can always do more later.

Above all, be humble. Be a learner. It's not just that there's more to know (there is), but there's a lot of growing into what you already know – beyond shallow application, to depth.

For those who walk alongside Starters, keep directing their attention to Jesus. Let Jesus take them deeper. Let Jesus branch them out. Just as Starters can have a tendency to participate in everything all at once, we can heap a lot of information and responsibility on people before their roots can sustain it all. Jesus is the Centerpiece of our faith. He always must be. Help Starters see this by how you center your own life on Christ.

Similarly, help Starters understand the basics of the Christian faith well. Of all the things we *can know*, there are some things that orthodox Christians have agreed on across denominations and centuries. Many of these things are found in the creeds and the Gospel accounts of Jesus. Revisit the basics often.

Starters who have placed their faith in Jesus and have

accepted Christian orthodoxy should be baptized and brought into the life of the Church as soon as possible.

And be prepared to walk with Starters through any early struggles. We know that life in this world as a Christian is not an easy life. Jesus said that in this world, we will have troubles, but he has overcome the world (John 16:33). Until roots have a chance to grow deeper, and experience catches up to reality, a Starter's faith can be easily uprooted. They may need to lean on your faith for a while.

THE EXPLORER STAGE

As for what was sown among thorns, this is he who hears the word, but the cares of the world and the delight in riches choke the word, and it proves unfruitful. (Matt. 13:22)

The third stage I see in this parable I call the Explorer. In our hiking illustration, the Explorer is the one who journeys onward into new territory. The Explorer understands the message of the Kingdom and has some depth. Explorers know the basics of orthodox Christianity well and hold Jesus central to life. The opportunity for these disciples is to move beyond borders and explore the frontiers of God's kingdom. They are discovering all the facets of their Christian identity and living into them. They are probing the layers of Kingdom culture and adapting. But there's a problem. Two 'weeds' threaten to choke the life out of their faith. One weed is the distractions of this world. Some of these distractions come in the form of a rapid-fire news cycle: politics, economics, climate, and violence. Other distractions can be more subtle: family demands, sports, career opportunities, and hobbies. Whatever the distractions, if not monitored, they can choke faith. The other weed that threatens faith is a preoccupation with accumulating wealth, a bias toward comfort. A life of faith will disrupt comfort.

As churches that minister to Explorers, how can we build a culture that makes room for genuine faith – trust (in God) that's able to take a step? The best way to help Explorers move deeper into the Kingdom is to set them in a community that looks like his kingdom. The rhythms we keep, our response to enemies and world events, our embrace of people at the margins of society, our readiness to follow God into uncomfortable places, and our alignment with the life and teachings of Jesus – all communicate as much as the Sunday message. Likely more.

If you see yourself as an Explorer, be sure to explore! Identify as an inhabitant of a whole new realm – God's kingdom. You are being fashioned by God and his Church to flourish here. Learn who God says you are. Figure out from Jesus how his kingdom operates. Get to know your King. Don't settle for an encampment at the border. Go deep in and prosper.

Get to know others who are on the same journey. Find out what you have in common. What experiences in the Kingdom do you share? Then exchange discoveries that seem different. What have you witnessed that others have not? What have they seen that you haven't? Learn how to travel together with people different from you.

Keep an eye on the two 'weeds'. Watch out for worldly distractions. Limit your news intake. Budget your finances. Regulate your consumption and production of social media. Manage your calendar. Then monitor any resistance to growth, change, and participation in what God is doing. Where does comfort interfere with obedience? Sometimes it's hard to see these weeds in our own lives. It takes courage but invite trusted friends to help you spot them.

For those who guide Explorers, help them cultivate a Kingdom mindset. God's kingdom stands in contrast to the world. Its ways – its patterns – are entirely different. The disciple's objective is to become fluent in Kingdom culture while staying aware of the world's patterns.

Prepare Explorers for spiritual conflict. The Enemy comes to steal, kill, and destroy. He will lie, accuse, confuse, and distract. He will exploit anxiety, disappointment, weariness, and shame. At the same time, he will try to blur the lines between the two kingdoms. Help Explorers see that a disciple's battle gear is not like the world's. Ours looks like truth, justice, righteousness, peace, faith, salvation, God's message, and prayer. Train them to engage the Enemy of our souls using these weapons.

And help Explorers see worldly distractions in their life and any bias toward comfort. As you do, be sure your motive is love and their best. This is never about doing more *for* God (or the church). It's about making space for their relationship *with* God and his leading in their life. Religious activity can become a weed – a distraction or a comfortable routine that chokes genuine faith.

THE VENTURER STAGE

As for what was sown on good soil, this is he who hears the word and understands it; he indeed bears fruit, and yields, in one case a hundredfold, in another sixty, and in another thirty. (Matt. 13:23)

The final stage I see in the parable, I call the Venturer. This hiker might be ready to become a guide – to form their LLC. The Venturer's life is marked by fruitfulness. Their roots run deep into a rich soil that's (at least relatively) free of weeds. No problems with this stage, right? Well, actually, there *are* some complications. Fruitful ministry can be thrilling. But it can also be tiring, frustrating, and discouraging. Bearing fruit takes a lot of energy. And while there may be seasons to fruitfulness, there's never a finish line. Even when things look great, we know God will periodically prune us to make us even more fruitful.

As churches with Venturers, how can we build a culture that celebrates produce without driving productivity? Fruitfulness is the byproduct of other things. And it's God's grace. How can we encourage the entire church to enrich, nourish, plant, water, and pray so that more fruit might emerge?

If you are a Venturer, shift your gaze from the fruit and focus on your depth. Fruit should be the natural product (produce) of a plant that's well tended. So, as far as it's up to you, tend to your life with God.

Remain humble. Humility is needed in every stage but maybe, especially for Venturers. Someone else planted Kingdom life in you. Others have watered that life along the way. And God has brought your growth. So, God and many people are stakeholders in your fruitfulness.

Surround yourself with other fruitful people. Not to compare. Not to compete. But to share what's hard and what's hopeful. Nothing trite. No clichés. But psalms, hymns, and spiritual songs – the Spirit's lyrics of real life.

For those helping Venturers along, find fruitful ministry and support it. Fruitful ministry can look like many things. It might look like making new disciples – what we usually think of. But it might look like training or care. Sometimes it looks like beauty brought into the world's messiest, most challenging places. Train yourself to see it, then help out. Give time. Give money. Offer a place to gather. Rally your personal network. Whatever is helpful.

Encourage fruitful ministry. This is different from support. It's about giving courage. Ministry is hard. People don't always respond as we'd like. The magnitude of need is usually far greater than our supply. Some people work in spiritually dark places and physically challenging spaces. Sometimes, the spirit is willing, but the flesh is weak. In these situations, loneliness and isolation work as misery magnifiers. Your presence and encouragement might be the difference between people continuing on and giving up.

Offer accountability. Venturers can become spiritually complacent and coast on ministry momentum. They might need someone like you to remind them to tend to their spiritual condition and protect their godly character. Far too many ministers start well, see fruitfulness, then self-destruct. This is preventable. And many times, prevention comes through the help of a true friend.

FROM STAGE TO STAGES

When we think about stages, we tend to think sequentially. Start with Stage 1, then move from Stage 1 to Stage 2, from Stage 2 to Stage 3, and so on. But with *our* stages – drawn from this parable of Jesus – I'd like you to see them as cumulative. We begin as a Seeker but end up a Seeker plus Starter plus Explorer plus Venturer. We never stop being Seekers. We don't cease to be Starters. We continue to Explore even as we see evidence of fruit. On our way to becoming trail guides, we hike the trail over and over again. Each time is a different experience, and we gain wisdom.

Maybe it's helpful to use the word *stage* another way – to see stages as platforms or arenas where we live our lives. There are messages of the Kingdom we still need to receive and understand. There are places where we need depth. There are times – lots of times probably – that we need to probe further while clearing our lives of distractions and a tendency toward spiritual stagnation. And there are opportunities for fruitful ministry.

Each stage has a set – a context. Our churches should provide the conditions for helping disciples grow and develop on every stage. Seekers need a set. Starters need a set. Explorers explore in a particular context. And there's a set that's helpful for Venturers too.

We grow to operate on four stages. Jesus tells us to ask, seek, and knock. He tells us to seek first God's kingdom and his righteousness. In Acts, we're told we should seek God in the hopes that we'll find him, even though he's not far from us. The message of God's kingdom (seed) is as vast as his kingdom. There's always more to receive and to understand. Those who have – those who live into what they've already been given – will receive more. What is God's message to you right now? What do you need to receive and take hold of before the Enemy comes and takes it away? If you're not sure, seek. Ask God. Is your community a seeking community?

Eugene Peterson said: *"There are no experts in the company of Jesus. We are all beginners."* [2] Compared to God's perspective, ours is small. We think we know more than we do. We suppose that our roots are deeper than they are. How often do we get rattled by trivial circumstances, let alone bigger things? Our faith is tested, and in our shallowness, we take back control. But God intends for difficult circumstances to deepen us. Look at the apostle Paul's words:

> we rejoice in our sufferings, knowing that suffering produces endurance, and endurance produces character, and character produces hope (Rom. 5:3-4)

I picture this as a moving sidewalk. From suffering to endurance to character to hope. Do you want to grow? Stay rooted in Christ during hard times. I'm still a Starter. We're all Starters. You and I need the depth that comes from real life in God's presence. Are we part of a community that values this kind of depth?

We are all still learning who we are in Christ. We're all still discovering what the culture of God's kingdom is like. Of course, it's one thing to discover and learn. It's quite another thing to adapt – to live into our new identity and culture. To become fluent. Then there are the weeds. Even when we find good soil and live in the potential of fruitfulness, the menace of weeds is always present. The cares, affairs, and distractions of this world are never far away. At the same time, comfort beckons us – especially when we get tired or discouraged. But we must be pioneers with machetes. How can we discover more of God and his kingdom? Is your community a place to ask questions and explore? Are you encouraged to clear space for God to grow your faith?

Ultimately, we want our lives to be fruitful – to nourish others and contribute to their flourishing. And we hope God's message in us will multiply itself in others a hundredfold, sixty, or thirty. Whatever influence we have on others comes from our understanding of God's revelation, our depth, and our exploration of the Kingdom and its King. Do you observe fruitfulness in your life personally and together with others? Does your community celebrate Spiritual fruit?

As a Seeker, seek to understand. As a Starter, seek and grow deeper. As an Explorer, seek, start, explore, and combat faith-choking weeds. And as a Venturer, do all these things as you bear fruit by God's grace.

How is it with you? Here's an invitation to Take a Zero and assess where you are, where you've come from, and where you're headed. Mark your map. Create a spiritual travelog and write.

---

[2] Eugene Peterson, *The Jesus Way: A Conversation on the Ways Jesus Is the Way*

PART 2

IMAGINING *the* GAUGES
of DISCIPLESHIP

In Part 1 of this book, I used the Parable of the Sower/ Soils to imagine stages of discipleship. Stages help us discern where disciples might be in our journey and what we might need there. We saw that the stages are cumulative and become four platforms for our spiritual life.

In Part 2, we look at gauges of discipleship. These are different indicators for taking stock of our progress in the Kingdom individually and collectively. People involved in discipleship can have difficulty gauging effectiveness and growth. We feel we should be monitoring something, but monitoring the *right* things seems beyond our reach. So, we're left watching what we can. Some of the more measurable things are seen in these questions:

- How regularly do we attend church?
- How much do we give financially?
- In what ways do we serve our church?
- Are we in a small group? And how well do we participate?
- How many Bible verses have we memorized?
- How many studies have we completed?
- How are we doing with quiet times? Are we on a streak?

We know these don't measure spiritual formation. But we do believe that – as habits – they can foster discipleship and spiritual growth. It's sort of like measuring our *physical* health. We don't know how to do it. But we can measure sleep, BMI, diet, and exercise – knowing that these generally *contribute* to good health.

Keeping with the health analogy, we can measure other things too: temperature, blood pressure, heart rate, cholesterol and triglycerides, blood sugar, blood oxygen saturation, EKG intervals, blood cell counts, etc. These aren't direct measures of health either. But they go beyond habits and give us some useful *indicators* of health.

Habits like church attendance, small groups, quiet time, and giving are helpful. They can influence our spiritual health. But while disciplines like these can foster spiritual formation, they aren't *measures* of formation. We aren't spiritually mature just because we go to church, enroll in studies, and quote scripture. Might we find other signals that give us more information, even if they're not precise or direct measures? When it came time to choose a king for Israel, God told Samuel:

> "Do not look on his appearance or on the height of his stature, because I have rejected him; for the Lord sees not as man sees; man looks on the outward appearance, but the Lord looks on the heart." (1 Samuel 16:7)

God looks on the heart. We cannot. We are left with monitoring outward expressions. And some expressions are better indicators of the heart than others. Remember, Jesus said our love for one another, and bearing good fruit, would reveal something about us. Conversely, adherence to Jewish law seemed to be a less reliable indicator. Quoting Isaiah, Jesus said to the Pharisees: "This people honors me with their lips, but their heart is far from me." (Matt. 15:8).

The gauges I'm about to introduce are indicators like temperature and blood pressure. They aren't direct measures of spiritual growth and health, but they focus on expressions more likely to reveal the heart. Like health, the disciple's formation isn't linear. There are ups and downs – frequent shifts in momentum. These gauges give us a way to pay attention to what's happening in our souls.

FIVE STATEMENTS AND A QUESTION

Here are five statements offered as gauges of formation:

1. God is great. God is good. And God is near. (Humility Gauge)

2. We are faithful stewards of the many forms of God's grace. (Responsibility Gauge)

3. People like us do things like this.[3] Or, As God's treasured possession, we live Jesus-like lives. (Acclimation Gauge)

4. We so love the world that we give our first and our best. (Imitation Gauge)

5. Our everyday story is for God's glory. (Mission Gauge)

The big question for each one is this: How real is this statement becoming in my actual lived life? Or for communities of believers: How real is this statement becoming in our actual lived life together?

---

[3] Adapted from Seth Godin, *This Is Marketing*, ©2018

I SURRENDER ALL

In Romans 12:1, the apostle Paul instructs us to present our bodies as a living sacrifice, holy and acceptable to God, which is our spiritual worship. When we become followers of Jesus – when we come to see him as King and give him our allegiance – we're giving him our all. Right now, I hear this hymn in my head. You too?

> All to Jesus I surrender,
> All to Him I freely give;
> I will ever love and trust Him,
> In His presence daily live.
> I surrender all,
> I surrender all.
> All to Thee, my blessed Savior,
> I surrender all.[4]

I surrender all. We surrender all. We say this and sing this as an aspirational confession. But if we perceive 'all' to mean perfection, we will live our lives afraid that we never quite measure up. So many people see struggle as failure. I think it's the *absence* of struggle that's failure. In spiritual formation, the way forward is challenging. It's self-denial.

It's every day cross-carrying. It's adapting to a whole new kingdom that's foreign to the world and our flesh. But God's grace is sufficient. His power is made complete in our weakness (2 Cor. 12:9).

With these gauges, I ask that you perceive 'all' to mean *Actual Lived Life*. What else do we have to surrender – to give? When we give our Actual Lived Life to Jesus, we give him our days and moments, our successes, our failures, our brokenness, our hurts, our giftedness, our weakness, our true and false identities, our resources, our relationships, and more. We love him and trust him to conform us to himself. Jesus wants us as we are. He loves us as we are. No hiding. No pretense. Give him your Actual Lived Life – your ALL. These gauges give us ways to see change and position ourselves for even more change. The question we bring to each is: "How real is this gauge – its statement – becoming in my (or our) Actual Lived Life?"

[4] Judson W. Van de Venter, 1896

THE HUMILITY GAUGE

God is great. God is good. And God is near.

> A night sky filled with stars.
> A sunrise at sea.
> A baby's bright eyes.
> A deciduous woods clothed in Autumn colors.
> A season of distress.
> A person's peace – even joy – in the midst of suffering.
> A song.
> What is it that turns your attention to God?

In the year 397, St. Augustine wrote: *"You have made us for yourself, O Lord, and our heart is restless until it finds its rest in you."* [5] We are a people with restless hearts. And we've forgotten where to turn for rest. God created us to be dependent on him. Our rest is found in trusting the One who is trustworthy. Jesus said: *"Come to me, all who labor and are heavy laden, and I will give you rest."* (Matt. 11:28). He said that trusting in his words is like building a house on a rock – a secure foundation able to withstand life's storms (Matt. 7:24-27).

Life does have its storms. To endure – to flourish even – we need to know that we know – *we really know* – that God is who he says he is. *God is great. God is good. And God is near.* Do you hear the child's mealtime prayer in this statement? The Kingdom of God belongs to people with childlike faith. Can we – with an honest, simple faith – rest our lives on God's greatness? God is all-powerful. God is all-knowing. God is from everlasting to everlasting. The foolishness of God is wiser than men, and the weakness of God is stronger than men (1 Cor. 1:25).

> Thine, O Lord, is the greatness, and the power, and the glory, and the victory, and the majesty; for all that is in the heavens and in the earth is thine; thine is the kingdom, O Lord, and thou art exalted as head above all (1 Chronicles 29:11).

Jesus said to his disciples: "All authority in heaven and on earth has been given to me." How real is God's greatness becoming in your actual lived life?

Can we – with childlike faith – rest our lives on God's goodness? O taste and see that the Lord is good! Happy is the man who takes refuge in him! (Ps. 34:8). O give thanks to the Lord, for he is good; for his steadfast love endures for ever! (Ps. 107:1). How real is the certainty of God's goodness becoming in your actual lived life?

And can we – with childlike faith – rest our lives on God's nearness to us? In the dinnertime prayer, a child prays, "let us thank him for our food". The God who spoke the universe into existence supplies the food on our table. "Look at the birds of the air: they neither sow nor reap nor gather into barns, and yet your heavenly Father feeds them. Are you not of more value than they?" (Matt. 6:26). How real is God's nearness becoming in your actual lived life?

"From one man, he made every nation of mankind to live over the entire face of the earth. He determined the appointed times and the boundaries where they would live. He did this so they would seek God and perhaps reach out for him and find him, though he is not far from each one of us." (Acts 17:26-27)

A child's prayer, so simple and familiar, is so profound, so significant to life. Its truth orients us to rest. But this requires humility. The prayer ends with "Amen" – "So be it". Who do we really trust? Are our thoughts higher than God's? Are our ways higher than his? What about the thoughts and ways of friends, enemies, celebrities, political leaders, alarmists, bootstrappers, or populists?

"Blessed is the man who trusts in the Lord,
    whose trust is the Lord.
He is like a tree planted by water,
    that sends out its roots by the stream,
and does not fear when heat comes,
    for its leaves remain green,
and is not anxious in the year of drought,
    for it does not cease to bear fruit." (Jeremiah 17:7-8)

Our first statement. Our first gauge. Now Take a Zero. Pause to consider your walk with God. How real is this gauge becoming in your actual lived life? What about compared to a year ago? Three years ago? Five? God promises that when the storms come, when the sun swelters, when the year of drought arrives, those who are rooted in him will continue to flourish. What can you do to deepen your trust? Can you recall times when you experienced God's greatness, goodness, and nearness? Can you see evidence of his greatness, goodness, and nearness right now? Make time to see. Reflect on and record these things. How can you position yourself to grow even more in these areas?

[5] Augustine, *Confessions*, 1.1.1.

WEIGHT-BEARING

Before moving to the next gauge, let's take a moment to look at the *order* of the gauges. A few years ago, my wife and I took a short vacation. Our hotel had an option to pay a little extra for a high floor with a view. We paid the premium and headed for our room. Looking out the window to the left, we had a terrific view of a river. But looking to the right, I just had to laugh. We paid extra for a spectacular view of a construction site. In that moment, I noticed our 'premium view' was of a five-story structure. And that made me think about these gauges. I guess this is the sort of thing that happens when your ministry role is discipleship. What I saw in that building is what I see in the gauges too. To have a five-story structure, you must have five floors – all five floors matter. But the first floor bears the weight of the four floors above it – even though it's still a work in progress. The second floor holds the weight of three floors above it. And so on. The top floor is supported by all those beneath.

Try to see this in these gauges too. As I move on to the second gauge, hold in your mind that this gauge depends on the existence of the first – even though the first gauge is still a work in progress. This will be true for all the gauges. Our fifth gauge is supported by all those before it. If the lower floors – the more foundational gauges – are weak, the whole structure can collapse. With this in mind, let's continue to the second gauge.

THE RESPONSIBILITY GAUGE

We are faithful stewards of the many forms of God's grace.

Sitting atop the Humility Gauge is the Responsibility Gauge. Any responsibility that we carry rests on the reality that God is great, God is good, and God is near. His greatness, goodness, and presence hold our responsibility and make it bearable – even satisfying. Our responsibility is just to be faithful stewards of God's manifold grace.

Before looking at our stewardship, let's see God's grace. I define grace this way:

> Grace is the unmerited God-given desire, ability, and resources to participate in our Father's economy (purpose, plan, activity) as His beloved.

Grace is a gift. It's everything we've received from God that we haven't earned. Scripture tells us that even our desire for God is his gift to us. Our mortal life and our next breath are his gifts. His presence with us; his image in us; the stability he gives; the scriptures; our relationships; our time, money, and resources; our identity; citizenship in his kingdom; adoption into his family; spiritual gifts; God's Creation and the senses we've been given to enjoy his creation; forgiveness and everlasting life. We've earned none of these – these and so many others. They are God's gifts – his grace.

God's gifts of grace are for us to enjoy. But they're not to be taken for granted or misused. We aren't entitled to them. We have received these gifts from a God who is great, good, and near – the God who spoke the universe into existence and upholds Creation by his powerful word! We receive all these gifts considering the character and intent of the Giver. Remember God's promise to our spiritual ancestor Abram: you will be blessed to be a blessing to all the nations on earth (Gen. 12:2).

God's gifts come with a responsibility. We are to be faithful stewards. Think back to the Garden of Eden. Man and Woman together were given an assignment – to exercise dominion over God's Creation. To tend it and care for it. That commission hasn't expired. A steward is a manager or administrator of another's property. We see God's gifts as things we can enjoy as we administer them on his behalf – honoring the Giver's intent.

We are faithful stewards of the many forms of God's grace. Take a Zero. Pause to think about God's gifts to you and your stewardship of those gifts. How real is this gauge becoming in your actual lived life? How aware are you of the many forms of God's grace in your life? Have you received and taken hold of those gifts? How faithfully do you administer his gifts?

THE ACCLIMATION GAUGE

People like us do things like this. Or, *As God's treasured posses-sion, we live Jesus-like lives.*

The third gauge – which rests on Humility and Responsibility – is Acclimation. Acclimation is about assimilating or adapting to newness.

> [The Father] has rescued us from the power of darkness and transferred us into the kingdom of his beloved Son, in whom we have redemption, the forgiveness of sins. (Col. 1:13-14)

> Therefore, if any one is in Christ, he is a new creation; the old has passed away, behold, the new has come. (2 Cor. 5:17)

We have been rescued and resettled in the kingdom of Christ. Everything is new. And we know from experience that, at first, new is *new*! We must acclimate to a lot of newness:

> For those who are in Christ Jesus,
> a new heart. A new spirit.

a new citizenship. A new family.
a new Sovereign and Father.
a new identity and culture.

That's what this gauge is about: acclimating to our new identity and culture.

People like us. God's treasured possession. Followers of Jesus have a new identity. We are a holy people, saints, the righteousness and justice of God, a priesthood, Jesus' bride, God's sons and daughters, forgiven, accepted by God, unconditionally loved, and more. That's a lot to adapt to, and it's a life-long process. How real are these identity markers becoming in your actual lived life? You are not your past failures. You are not your past abuse. You are not what friends and family, enemies, bullies, mean girls, trolls, and others say you are. You are who God says you are. Your identity is a *received* identity – received from God. Take a Zero. Pause to consider your true self. Are you better able to live in your new identity than before? If so, that's progress. You are acclimating.

Do things like this. Live Jesus-like lives. Followers of Jesus have a new culture. Jesus came to rescue us from the dominion of darkness. Let's pause and dwell on that. The word *rescue* suggests that we were held captive. The word *dominion* says that we were held captive by a governance, a ruler, an authority. That ruler defined a culture that we were held captive in. That *was* our culture – our way of life. The word *rescue* also tells us that we needed to be rescued. We were in a place that we didn't belong. But the Father rescued us. That rescue meant Jesus – Immanuel, God with us – had to go to the Cross. There he was humiliated, tortured, and murdered. He did that for us – for our rescue. How humbling it is to receive this incredible gift of God's grace.

It gets better. The Father didn't just rescue us. He transferred us. He resettled us. Maybe you remember a movie called *The Terminal*. [6] The story goes like this. Victor Navorski (Tom Hanks) is from a politically unstable country. He flies to the United States and lands at New York's JFK Airport. While in the air, there's a coup in his home country, and his passport is no longer accepted in the U.S. Victor can't enter the United States. And he has no home to return to. His only option is to live in the airport. How many believers know they've been rescued from the dominion of darkness just to live in a narrow space between two borders – waiting to be admitted to heaven someday?

This isn't what the apostle Paul is saying in Colossians. We were rescued from a place and admitted to another place, all at once. This other place is the kingdom of God's Son. We've already seen that our identity has changed – a new citizenship and passport of sorts. This new kingdom also comes with a new culture. It's a culture that could not be more contrary to the culture we were rescued from. Everything is new, and we need to acclimate. By demonstration, teaching, and storytelling, Jesus described the culture of his kingdom. Just look at his Sermon on the Mount found in Matthew 5-7. Some see this as an impossible standard that no one can live up to. I see it as a description of his kingdom. Some live outside this kingdom. To them, it's all foolishness. Some are recent migrants to his kingdom. To them, Jesus' description seems beautiful but still very new and foreign. Then some have been journeying in his kingdom for a while. What Jesus describes in his 'sermon' is starting to feel like home to them – even though they still bear traces of the old culture they were rescued from.

The apostle Paul reminds New Testament churches often that they used to be one way (old culture), but now they're different (new culture). Passages like Romans 12, Galatians 5, Ephesians 4, Colossians 3, and 1 Thessalonians 4 highlight these contrasts. The behavior of a Kingdom citizen should reflect the culture we call home. Behavior relates to belonging. Our quest is to become fluent in our new culture – and to let go of the old patterns.

What about you? Take a Zero. Pause to assess your fluency in Kingdom culture. How real are the patterns of God's Kingdom becoming in your actual lived life? Are you able to see the differences between his kingdom and the world? How successful have you been at letting go of the cultural patterns of the world and embracing the ways of your new home? Acclimation is progress.

[6] *The Terminal*, Sept. 15, 2004, Written by Sasha Gervasi and Jeff Nathanson, Directed by Steven Spielberg, Distributed by Dreamworks

THE IMITATION GAUGE

We so love the world that we give our first and our best.

It's the most recognizable verse in the Bible. John 3:16. *For God so loved the world that he gave his only Son, that whoever believes in him should not perish but have eternal life.* God so loved the world that he gave. Our fourth gauge sits atop humility, responsibility, and acclamation. Humble before God, faithful stewards of his manifold grace, acclimating to our new identity and culture, now we love like God loves. We love by giving. Ephesians 5:1-2 reads:

> Therefore be imitators of God as beloved children. And walk in love, as Christ loved us and gave himself up for us, a fragrant offering and sacrifice to God.

God is love (1 John 4:8). To be a citizen of his kingdom is to live by love. Love is the way of the Kingdom. We see love's prominence throughout the New Testament – from Jesus identifying love (of God) as the greatest commandment and love (of neighbor) as the second, to Jesus' expression of love on the Cross, to Paul's discourse on love in 1 Corinthians 13, to James' royal law of love. (James 2:8) It's hard to miss God's emphasis.

John 3:16 is about Jesus' love for the world. Jesus says it's only natural to love people who love you. Everyone can do that (Luke 6:32-33). But God showed his love for us in that while we were still sinners, Christ died for us (Rom. 5:8). Christ died for the righteous and the unrighteous (1 Pet. 3:18). God so loved the world – those who were still his enemies. Even on the Cross, Jesus appealed to the Father for the very people who were humiliating, torturing, and killing him: "Father forgive them; for they know not what they do." (Luke 23:34).

Therefore, be imitators of God. Looking again at John 3:16, we see God gave his *only* Son. The firstborn of all Creation (Col. 1:15) and the lamb without blemish or spot (1 Pet. 1:18-20). In the Old Testament, we see that God's people brought their first and their best for sacrifice. Jesus offering himself followed this same pattern.

We present our bodies as living sacrifices, holy and acceptable to God. This is our Spiritual worship (Rom. 12:1). Imitating God, we give the first and the best of our lives to God as worship. And imitating God, we so love the world that we give this way. We love and give for the sake of others – even those who mock our Father and us.

We so love the world that we give our first and our best. Take a Zero. Pause to reflect on your love for God and others. How real is this gauge becoming in your actual lived life? Sometimes it's hard to love people close to us. It's harder still to love some people in our churches. Loving neighbors can be hard. Loving enemies is extremely hard. But this is the way of God's kingdom – the kingdom we have been resettled in. Is this more of a reality in your life now than in times past? Progress.

THE MISSION GAUGE

Our everyday story is for God's glory.

Sitting atop all the others is our fifth gauge: the Mission Gauge. I write in an American context. We are doers. We value productivity. Results! We are encouraged to be purposeful, missional. These are all good things, but they are the top floor, not the foundation. Whether within our churches or beyond, we should participate with humility before God. We are faithful stewards of God's grace. We're being formed into our new identities and culture. And we're imitators of God, loving the world as he does. Every floor is still under construction, but they're all in place. Our work in the world is an expression of what God is doing in our own souls.

The Mission Gauge is about story. Our story. It's about how God is revealed in the tapestry of our life. No thread is wasted. We know that in everything, God works for good with those who love him, who are called according to his purpose (Rom. 8:28).

We live as Kingdom citizens in many different spheres: church, home, the workplace, the marketplace, community service, politics, and play. With the other four gauges in place, now we can look for ways to be salt, light, yeast, and a fragrance of the knowledge of Christ.

Maybe you're like me. I must often be reminded that the world's fate does not depend on me. It is God who spoke Creation into existence. It is God – specifically, Jesus – who upholds the universe by his powerful word (Heb. 1:3). God is sovereign over all. Whatever happens in each of my daily domains, the most powerful Being in the universe has allowed it. The question for me – for us – is will we be ambassadors of his kingdom in these domains as they are? Will we represent the interests of his kingdom right here, right now? Steven Garber asks: "Can you know the world and still love it?" [7]

In trying to make my world more Kingdom-like, it can sometimes seem that nothing works. In desperation, I pray. But Rick, that's so backward! Trust God and pray *first*! In many situations, we won't be able to do anything more than pray. In prayer, God might show us creative ways to use our influence to bend culture toward his kingdom. Or he may act in some other manner entirely.

In Jeremiah 29, we read about God's people in exile. Through the prophet Jeremiah, God tells his people to: "seek the welfare of the city where I have sent you into exile, and pray to the Lord on its behalf, for in its welfare you will find your welfare." (Jer. 29:7) Our comfort is not the primary motivation here. God blesses us to be a blessing to others (Gen. 12:2). But generally, if we work for the welfare of the people around us, we will participate in that welfare.

We who work for the world's welfare act like a covering of salt, a glow of light, a pinch of yeast, or a pleasing fragrance. These biblical metaphors suggest an approach that is creative, patient, and subversive. Sometimes our work for others' welfare might not even be observable. In a culture built on deception and lies, we can prove ourselves authentic and trustworthy. In a culture of greed, we can be generous. In a world that divides and scatters, we can be the people who gather and pursue justice. Among people committed to violence, we can be the ones who seek peace and pursue it (1 Pet. 3:11).

Hard as it is to remember, we are not contending against flesh and blood but against principalities and powers (Eph. 6:12). Our weapons are not the weapons of this world (1 Cor. 10:4). We fight spiritual battles against unseen enemies, with divine weapons. Warfare waged in the Spirit serves up Spiritual fruit: love, joy, peace, patience, kindness, goodness, faithfulness, gentleness, and self-control.

Our mission as ambassadors of God's kingdom is to try to bend the culture of every one of our domains towards Kingdom flourishing. Nudge our churches toward holiness. Nudge our households toward stability and unconditional love. Nudge our workplaces toward human dignity. We're in this for the long haul until every knee bows, and every tongue confesses that Jesus is Lord (Phil. 2:9-11).

Our everyday story is for God's glory. How about you? Take a Zero. Pause to see how God uses you to represent his kingdom in all your life's circles. Are you living your life in a way that bends culture toward his kingdom? Are you able to release control to God? Are you bringing humility, stewardship of God's grace, your God-given identity and culture, and love to your ministry efforts? If these are more real in your actual lived life now than they were in the past, celebrate!

[7] Steven Garber, *Visions of Vocation: Common Grace for the Common Good*

A DASHBOARD

Dashboards have become a regular part of life. Once a thing of cars and airplanes, now we have dashboards in our workplaces and on our phone apps. Dashboards present us with the essential gauges in one place. The dashboard's gauges bring focus and help us see historical trends. What if *our* five gauges could serve as a spiritual formation dashboard? Might these gauges bring focus to how I *train myself and others to be trained by Christ* (my definition of discipleship)? And can they give me a way to reflect on how things are changing over time?

- What do I believe about God enough to anchor my life in him?

- Am I taking hold of God's gifts to me? How well am I administering his grace?

- Who am I *really*? Who does God say I am? Am I becoming more like *that* person?

- How does God's kingdom operate? Am I becoming more fluent in *that* culture?

- How Christlike am I in my self-denying love for others – neighbors and even enemies?

- How well does my everyday life reveal God to the world? Do my attitudes, actions, and prayers tip the atmosphere of my various domains toward heaven?

Each of these questions is processed through the lens of our Actual Lived Life. These same questions can also be asked of our families, groups, and churches. Like blood pressure, these gauges don't hold steady. My blood pressure can change dramatically in one day! And these gauges don't always trend in one direction. But they do offer a way to celebrate God's work in us and position ourselves for more of his work.

SPIRITUAL HEALTH AND WELLNESS

Returning to our physical health analogy, one criticism people have of the American healthcare system is that it places more emphasis on treating disease than on promoting health and wellness. We wait until a problem surfaces, then we attack it. I can't say whether or not that's a fair critique, but the question might prompt us to consider our *spiritual* health and wellness. Christians seem pretty good at spotting sin and brokenness in others. And we readily offer all sorts of *treatments*. But what if we gave more attention to spiritual fitness? I've been told the best way to manage weeds is to keep my grass healthy. A dense, thriving turf is an inhospitable environment for weeds. Likewise, a life lived in God's company will be an inhospitable environment for sin.

Whether it's our physical health, the state of our yard, or our spiritual condition, we need to make some investments. We need good disciplines and rhythms. And we need to pay attention to indicators. For spiritual health, pray; learn to hear God's voice. Recognize his activity. Get to know his names and his character. Meet God in scripture and let him change your heart. See God in Jesus and imitate him. Then, periodically Take A Zero and look for change. Where you see growth, celebrate. And where you don't, adjust your rhythms and disciplines.

We are being fashioned to flourish in God's kingdom. Our quest is to become fluent in Kingdom culture. This means we come to know our King, and we trust him. He defines who we are, and we adjust. He establishes the cultural values that we live by. And we conform. For our formation, all eyes are on Jesus. He is our Ruler, Example, Teacher, Trainer, Encourager, Defender, and Intercessor. He is our Solid Foundation. It's Jesus who sent the Holy Spirit to be our Comforter, Helper, and Power – while pointing us back to Jesus. Dallas Willard said:

> "Discipleship is the process of becoming who Jesus would be if he were you."

To the degree that I am becoming the person Jesus would be if he were me is the degree to which I am being formed well. Same for you. And the same for our churches. This happens *in* stages and then *on* stages. And it can be tested with gauges. Stages and gauges imply process. And so does the word *becoming*. This is true for us, and it's true for others in our faith community.

Speaking of community, proper discipleship requires community. Disciples aren't formed well in isolation. We haven't been brought into some vague concept of the Kingdom of God. That would be more of a philosophy than a lived reality. We participate with actual people in an actual place at an actual time.

Our faith community isn't just a *chosen* community; it's also a *received* one. The community God gives us will have a variety of viewpoints, a range of abilities, and a spectrum of maturity. Our one defining hope is that we journey with people who have surrendered their ALL to Jesus and are becoming more fluent in his kingdom. I am making a case *for* local churches, small groups, discipleship bands, and accountability groups. Yes, we are part of Jesus' global Church, but that affiliation can remain impersonal, requiring very little of us. Commit to a real community of real people. They will be God's grace in your life just as you are in theirs. We are being formed personally in a community that's being formed together.

FINAL THOUGHTS FROM A FELLOW HIKER

A risk of writing books on discipleship and formation is that I am an actual person. That means some people who read this book know me. Some have known me in the past; other relationships are more current. Even with my blind spots, I can see how unChristlike I can be – especially at the heart level. I know my weaknesses, limitations, and fears – at least some of them. This book isn't written by someone who's arrived at a destination but by a fellow hiker with you.

In some areas, I'm still approaching the trailhead. There are things I don't understand. And to be honest, I can be slow to do anything about what I *can* understand. In other areas, I'm on the beginning of the trail – the steepest part. My faith doesn't always hold up well against gale-force winds and the sun's scorching heat. I tend to trust myself over God. In still other areas, I want to stop at a beautiful clearing (can you see the meadow and the pond?), then turn around and head back. But I know there's so much more to discover if I forge ahead, machete in hand. And thankfully, there are some areas where I can operate as a guide to others, drawing on my experience so far.

So far. The gauges show me that I have grown some over the years. When I make time – when I Take a Zero – I can see how each of the five gauge statements has become more real in my Actual Lived Life. Over days, weeks, and months the gauges can swing wildly. But looking back over decades, I can see a general trend in the right direction. I find this encouraging, even knowing I'm still a beginner. Now it's your turn. Make time to assess your position and progress. Get away periodically and prayerfully think about – write about – your life in terms of these stages and gauges.

I wish I could bring this bit of maturity I've gained to my next time around. But there is no next time around. Instead, I will bring what I have to the One who is Everlasting Life and lay my ALL at his feet. Thankfully I *can* share some of what I've gained with those coming behind, just as so many others have done for me. I pray you make your trip wisely and find great joy in it.

FORMATION LOOP TRAIL

... to share in a companionship of the saints,
with the Father and the Son,
where Kingdom life is becoming more normal, less foreign;
working for good in the world,
and recruiting one more disciple of Jesus ...
(repeat)

APPENDIX 1

Taking A Zero – Individuals, Families, and Groups

STAGES

1. Are you a Seeker? Are you presently seeking God and a fresh revelation of his kingdom? Is there anything he has shown you that you resist or don't understand? Are you open to understanding? Is your posture to take hold of God's message? Are you making efforts to understand? Who can you process with?

2. Are you a Starter? We can grow deeper in almost every area. But is there anything God is bringing to mind right now? Is there anything God has shown you that still sits on the surface? When you feel stressed or anxious, what happens to your rooted-ness? What tends to knock you down or uproot you? And what would help you hold onto Jesus, your foundation, during these storms of life?

3. Are you an Explorer? Are you pressing ever deeper into God's kingdom to discover God's character, his

vision for you, and his ways? Do you see his kingdom as your homeland? Are you aware of the world's distractions? How successfully can you resist those distractions and keep your focus on Christ? When obedience calls you to move beyond comfort, can you respond in faithfulness?

4. Are you a Venturer? Do you see evidence of Kingdom fruitfulness in your life? Are your life and words helping others follow Christ more faithfully? Have you been attentive to the condition of your own heart and growth, even as you have engaged in ministry activity?

GAUGES

Pick a point of reference from your past (one year, three years, five years) and consider these questions from your Actual Lived Life.

1. Humility. Can you see evidence in your life that reveals a growing confidence in God's greatness? God's Goodness? His nearness? Is God's presence your place of stability and rest in good and difficult times? Does your vision of his greatness mean you don't have to prove your own? Are you more able to trust that God is good even when bad things happen? Is it becoming easier to believe that God is near, hears you, and cares for you? Can you remember specific encounters with him that were faith-building?

2. Responsibility. Can you create (or add to) a list of examples of God's grace (gifts) to you? Are you

growing in your ability to see his grace? Is your awareness of God's grace bringing an increased sense of gratitude and less of a sense of entitlement? Can you identify ways you have grown in your faithful stewardship of the things on your list? How has your stewardship honored God's intent?

3. Acclimation. In what ways has God revealed false aspects of your identity and replaced them with his truth? Have you been able to live into what he says about you and give less weight to what others say (including yourself)? Are you more able to see God's image and dignity in other people? Have you grown in your understanding of the contrast between the ways of Christ and the ways of the world? And have you been able to release worldly patterns and embrace Kingdom ones instead?

4. Imitation. Can you see a shift in your heart from an 'against the world' posture toward a 'for the world' one? Can you think of specific ways you have shown love to people you wouldn't naturally be inclined to love? People in your church? Neighbors? Enemies?

5. Mission. Do the circles you run in experience God's goodness through you? Do they tilt a little bit more toward Kingdom culture due to your presence and influence? Do you bring the other gauges along when you share your beliefs as a Jesus follower or serve in a ministry capacity? Does your ministry align with your heart and soul?

APPENDIX 2

Taking A Zero – Ministries, Mentors, and Guides

STAGES

1. Seekers. Are you helping Seekers expand their concept of the message of the Kingdom? Can you help them see that those who have received – and are open to receiving – will receive more? Are you postured to help Seekers to understand, not just hear? Do you encourage questions and spiritual conversation? What would new Seekers experience in your culture?

2. Starters. Are you helping Starters reframe their understanding of depth – away from consumption to rootedness? Are you able to walk closely with Starters until they deepen? If necessary, can they draw on your faith for a time? Can you help people in tight theological boxes get 'repotted' so their roots might grow again? Can you encourage them to read widely and learn from others?

3.   Explorers. Are you helping people move on from the 'Christianity Border'? Can you help them explore more of the fullness of Christian life? Does your culture help people discover their true identity, and are they able to experience Kingdom life? Are Explorers encouraged to participate as part of a community of faith? Are you helping Explorers deal with the weeds of worldly distractions and a bias toward comfort?

4.   Venturers. Is produce celebrated over productivity? Are Venturers able to see that fruitful ministry comes by the Spirit, from abiding with Christ? Are there ways for Venturers to get to know each other and encourage one another? Are there places to freely share stories and hardships?

GAUGES

Pick a point of reference from your past (one year, three years, five years) and consider these questions from your corporate Actual Lived Life. Is your ministry growing in each of these areas?

1.   Humility. Can people see your ministry and its leaders embrace God's greatness, goodness, and nearness during good times and hard times? Do people see humility before God and others in the leaders and core? Does your ministry project a posture of reverence, wonder, and awe of God?

2. Responsibility. In your ministry, do people experience gratitude rather than entitlement? Do they see your ministry treat assets, relationships, and influence as God's grace? Do people see you as faithful stewards of these gifts?

3. Acclimation. Does your ministry see yourselves as a distinct, called-out people? Different from the world and its ways? Are you more concerned with becoming Christlike than criticizing people who don't follow Jesus? Can you leave the judgment of nonbelievers to God and look on them with Jesus-like compassion? Are you committed to pursuing Kingdom influence according to Kingdom ways?

4. Imitation. Do people experience love above all? Do you teach and demonstrate that everything must be done in love? Do people understand the difference between loving the world and loving its *ways*? Do your ministry and its leaders give your first and best, even as you encourage others to?

5. Mission. Does your culture celebrate fruitfulness resulting from spiritual vitality and God's grace? Is your ministry work undergirded by God-like love, a Kingdom orientation, faithful stewardship of God's grace, and humility in the presence of a great and good God? Do you operate as participants with God, by his leading?

AUTHOR BIO

Rick Shafer serves as a pastor and faith formation direc-tor at Port City Community Church in Wilmington, North Carolina. He and his wife Elizabeth were married in 1983. Together they are taking in all the joys of grandparenthood, thanks to two wonderful sons and daughters-in-law.

Rick was trained as a Chemical Engineer and has worked in the chemical and life science industries. He and his family also served in missions ministry for a season. His work experience includes process engineering, marketing, training, donor development, and member care.

Rick's first exposure to discipleship was with Word of Life (Schroon Lake, NY) in the 1970s. Since then, this discipleship interest has been developed and grounded through YWAM's Discipleship Training School and School of Evangelism, reading and study, experimentation, and practice.

Rick loves the outdoors – running, hiking, biking, and swimming. And he enjoys music, reading, writing, and a good conversation over coffee.